A KID'S GUIDE TO DIY

A BOOK OF CAMPING AND SURVIVAL PROJECTS

for Kids Who Love to Go Wild

Solar-powered oven

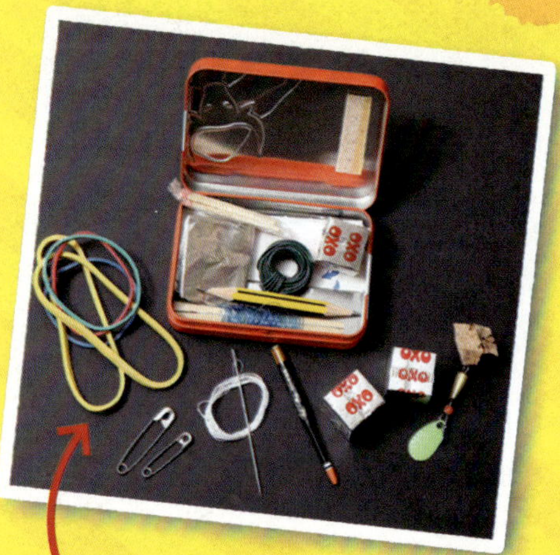

Mini survival kit

by Ruth Owen

WINDMILL BOOKS

Published in 2022 by Windmill Books,
an Imprint of Rosen Publishing
29 East 21st Street, New York, NY 10010

Produced for Rosen by Ruth Owen Books
Designer: Emma Randall
Photos courtesy of Ruth Owen Books and Shutterstock

Photo Credits:
Cover, 1, 5, 6–7, 8–9, 10–11, 13, 21, 22, 24–25, 26–27, 28–29 © Ruby Tuesday Books and John Such; cover, 1, 14, 16–17 © Emily Heath; 1, 4–5, 12–13, 15, 16–17, 18–19, 20–21, 22–23, 24, 27 © Shutterstock.

Cataloging-in-Publication Data

Names: Owen, Ruth.
Title: A book of camping and survival projects for kids who love to go wild / Ruth Owen.
Description: New York : Windmill Books, 2022. | Series: A kid's guide to DIY | Includes glossary and index.
Identifiers: ISBN 9781538270370 (pbk.) | ISBN 9781538270394 (library bound) | ISBN 9781538270387 (6 pack) | ISBN 9781538270400 (ebook)
Subjects: LCSH: Wilderness survival--Juvenile literature. | Camping--Juvenile literature.
Classification: LCC GV200.5 O94 2022 | DDC 613.6'9--dc23

Manufactured in the United States of America

CPSIA Compliance Information: Batch BSWM22: For Further Information contact Rosen Publishing, New York, New York at 1-800-237-9932

CONTENTS

WARNING
Neither the author nor the publisher shall be liable for any bodily harm or damage to property that may happen as a result of carrying out the projects in this book.

GET READY TO GO WILD!

Would you like to spend time outdoors? Maybe you want to go hiking in a forest or another wild place. Perhaps you are planning a camping trip with your family or friends. If so, then this book is perfect for you and will teach you lots of essential survival skills.

You will learn how to make a mini survival kit, build a shelter from branches and leaves, and even light a fire without using matches!

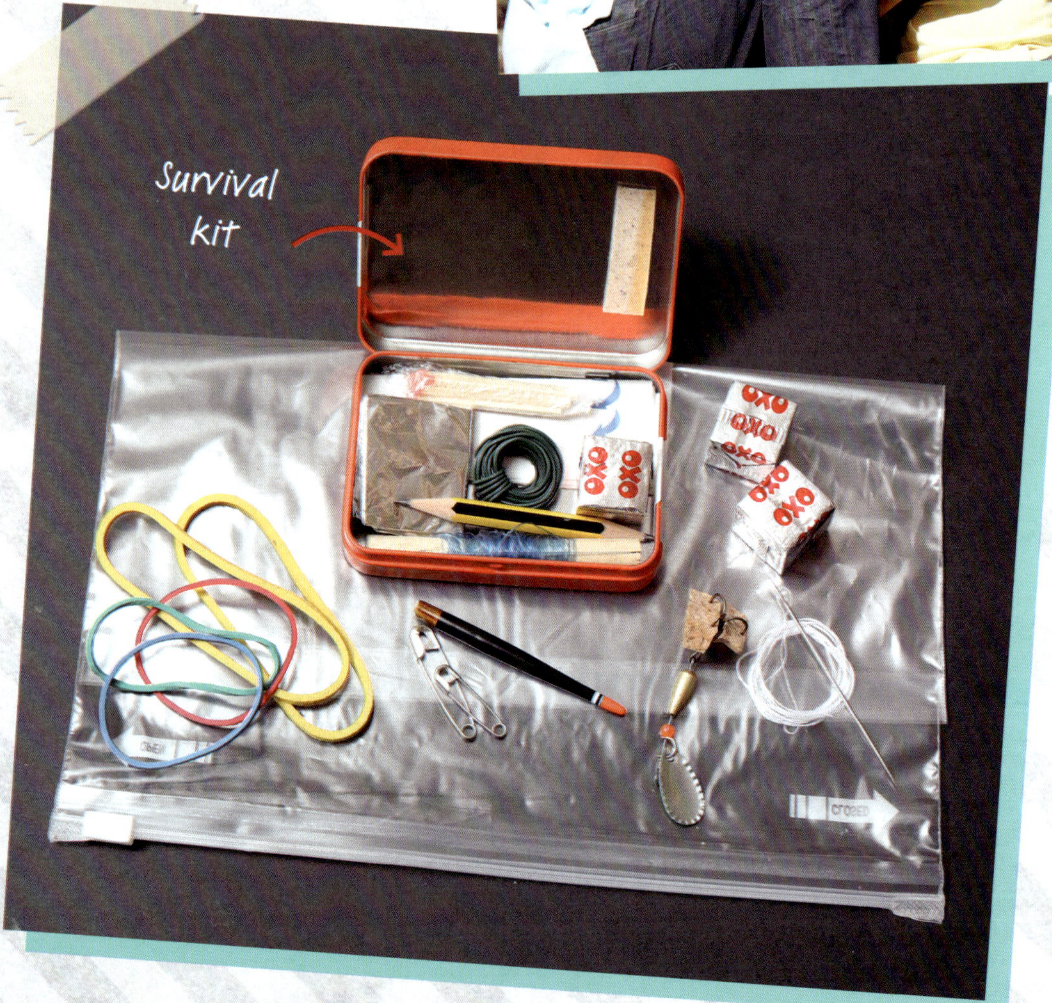

If hanging out with friends in your backyard is more your thing, there are fun projects that show you how to turn flowerpots into a cooler to keep your drinks chilled, and how to make an oven powered by the sun.

MINI SURVIVAL KIT

You've got your tent, sleeping bag, food, and water bottle all packed for your camping trip. But out in the **wilderness** unexpected things can sometimes happen.

Therefore, it's helpful to always carry a survival kit in your pocket. You can never **anticipate** what might go wrong, so pack your kit with lots of useful everyday items.

WARNING

Only use a glue gun or work with a craft knife and matches if an adult is there to help you.

On the next few pages, you will find suggestions for putting together a **survival kit**. Find ways to **utilize** every tiny bit of space inside the kit and include as many items as possible.

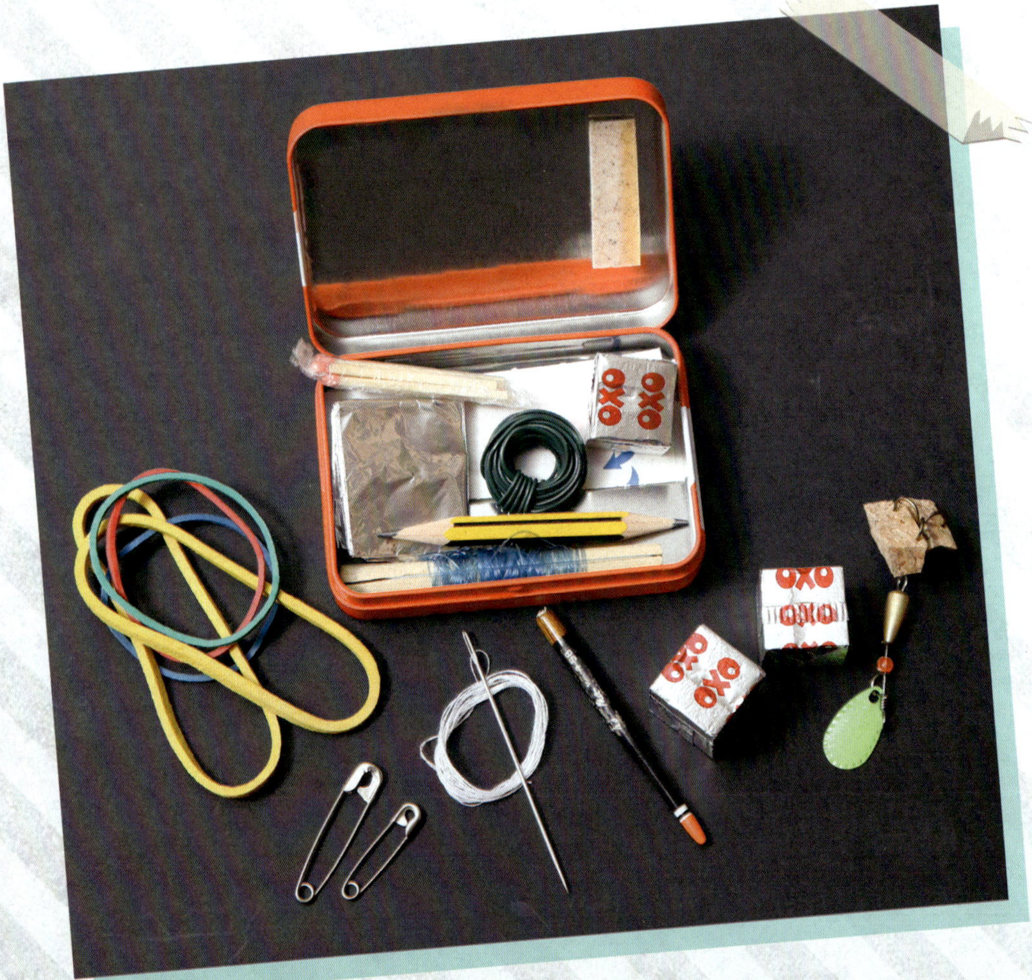

YOU WILL NEED:

- A small tin or plastic container
- Duct tape
- Scissors
- A glue gun
- A pencil sharpener
- Survival items for the kit as required

STEP 1: Find a pocket-sized plastic container or tin. The type of tin that holds mints works well. Then begin putting together the components of your survival kit.

STEP 2: To make a small but simple knife, take a craft knife blade and wrap one edge with duct tape. The duct tape makes a safe edge for holding.

STEP 3: For safety, but also to utilize every tiny bit of space inside the kit, tape the knife inside the box or tin's lid using duct tape.

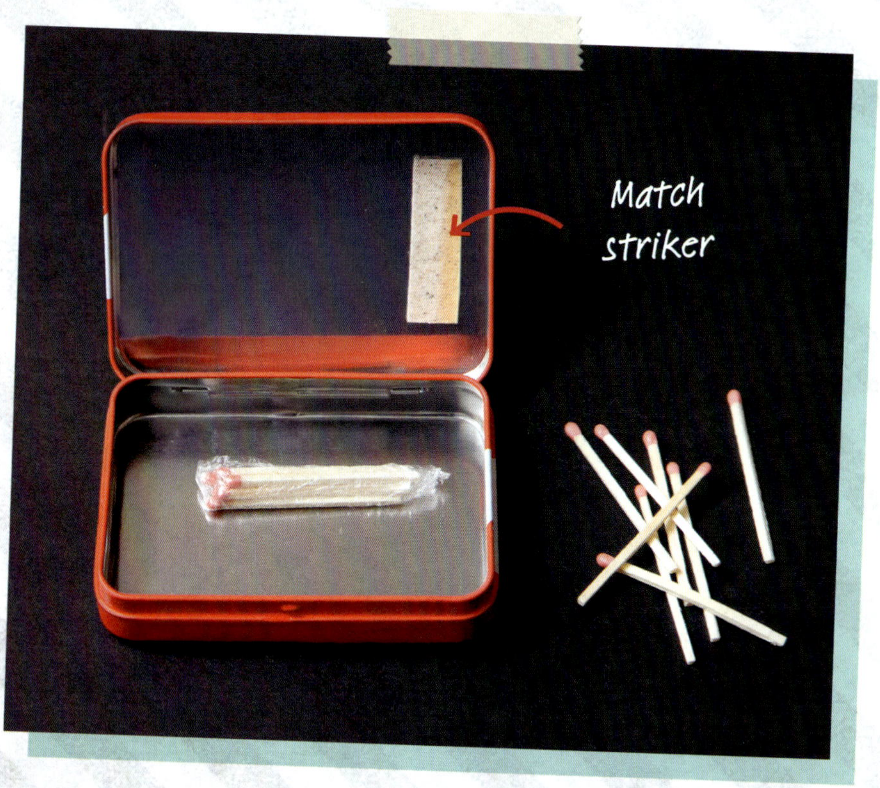

STEP 4: If you want to carry matches, glue the striker from a matchbook inside the lid of the box or tin. Tightly wrap some matches in plastic wrap to keep them dry.

STEP 5: A pencil could be useful, so snap a pencil into a short length that will fit inside your kit. Sharpen both ends.

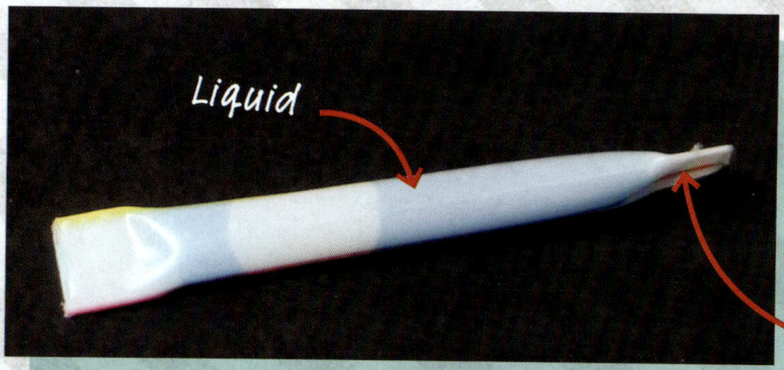

STEP 6: To make mini containers for holding antiseptic for cuts, hand cleanser, or other liquids, cut a drinking straw into short lengths. Place a blob of hot glue at one end of a straw, then squeeze the end of the straw so it seals up. Fill the straw with liquid, then seal the other end using hot glue.

STEP 7: If you will be near water, put together a basic selection of equipment for catching fish.

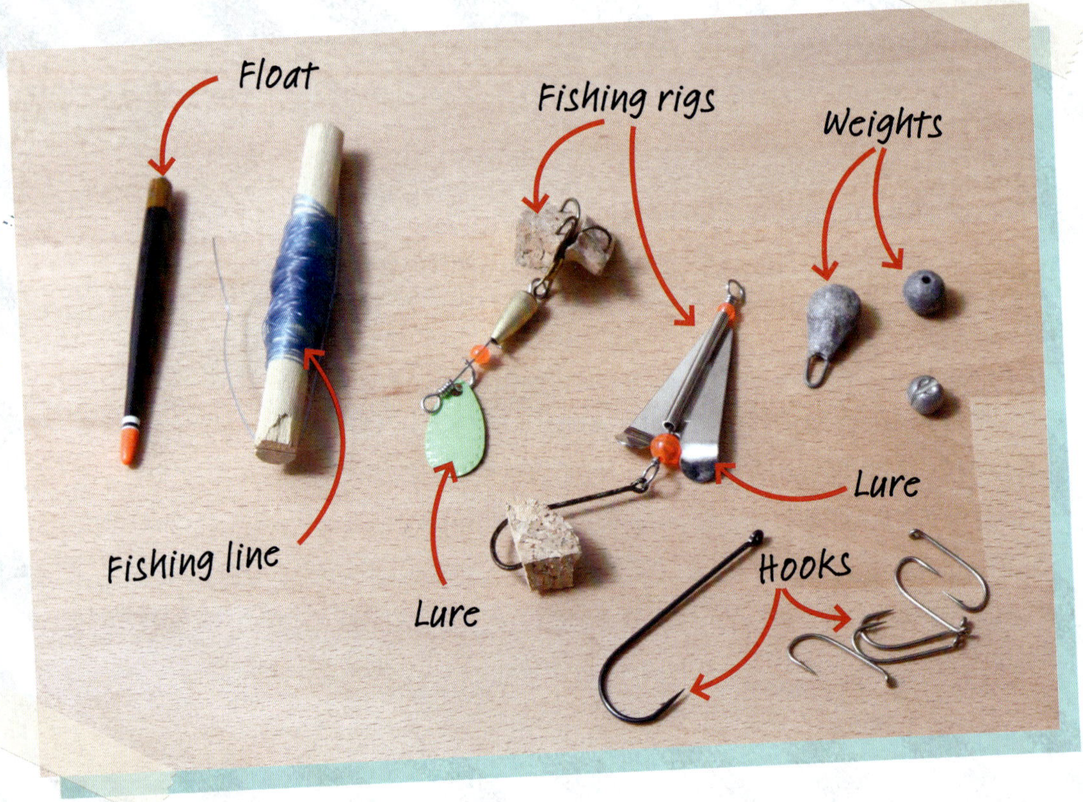

STEP 8:
A large sheet of aluminum foil can be used for collecting water or for wrapping around food so it can be cooked on an open fire.

STEP 9: Try to think of items that might be useful and fit as many as possible into your survival kit.

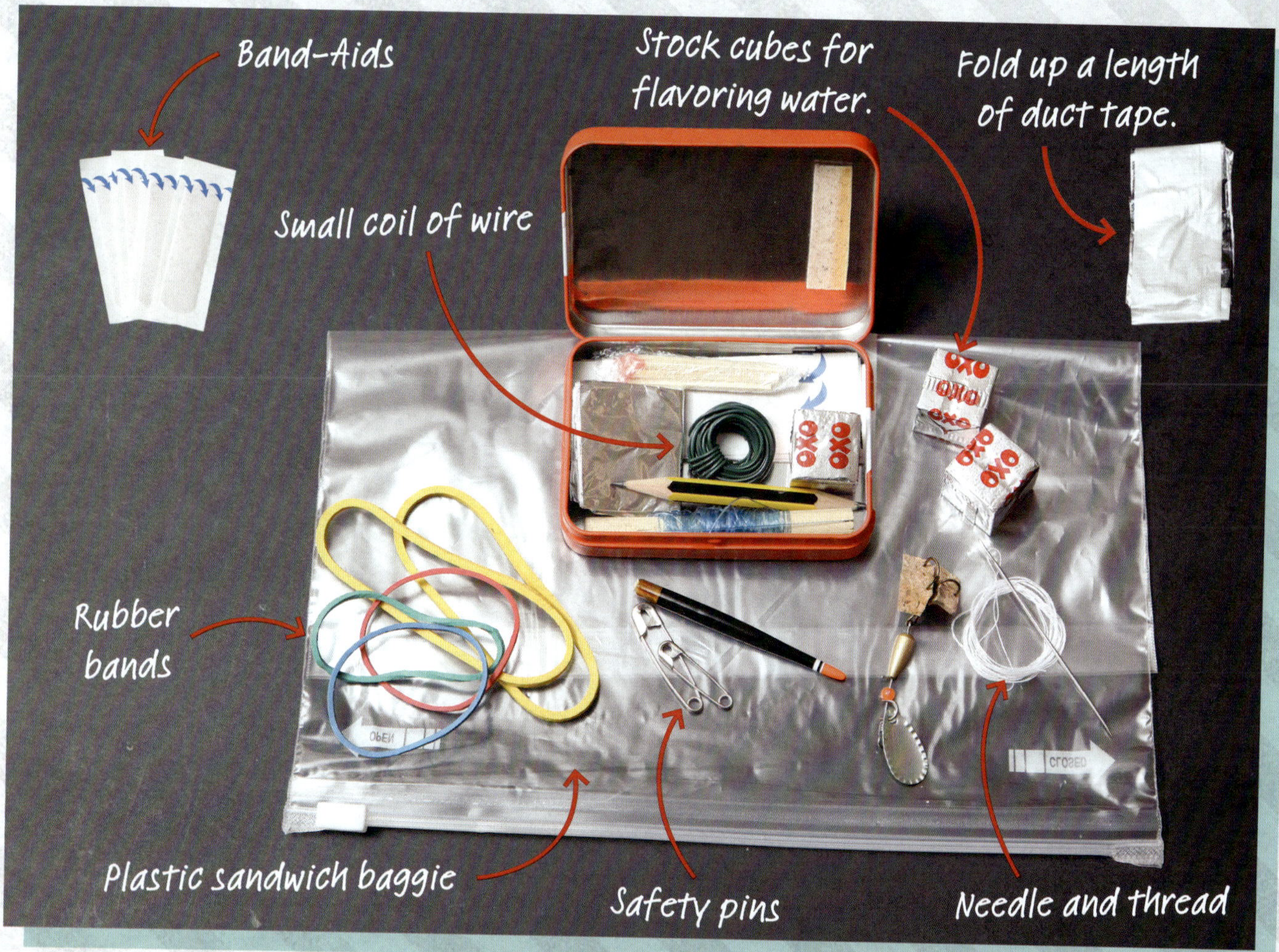

STEP 10: To save space inside the kit and to keep it secure, wrap the rubber bands around the outside of the box or tin.

NEEDLE COMPASS

A **compass** is a device that allows you to figure out if you are walking to the north, east, south, or west. This information is very important when you are spending time in a wilderness area.

No matter which direction you turn, the needle in a compass will always point north. This is because the needle is pulled to the north by the natural magnetism of the Earth. This will help you stay on a straight path and not walk around in circles if you are in an environment, such as a forest, where everything looks the same in all directions.

compass

You can add a tiny compass to your survival kit, or make your own using just some water, a leaf, a bar magnet, and a needle.

STEP 1: Place the needle on the magnet so its point is facing toward the magnet's south pole. Leave for an hour and the needle will become magnetized.

YOU WILL NEED:

- Some water
- A leaf
- A bar magnet
- A sewing needle

STEP 2: Find a small, flat leaf and some water, such as a puddle. Float the leaf on the puddle.

STEP 3: Gently place the magnetized needle onto the leaf.

Now that the needle is floating on water it can move freely. Like the needle in a compass, the Earth's magnetism will pull the point of the needle toward north. You need to use a leaf, like a raft, beneath the needle to stop the needle from sinking.

STEP 4: To be sure your leaf and needle compass is working, you can test it two or three times by gently moving the leaf with your finger so the needle is pointing in a different direction. Each time, the needle and leaf will slowly turn and come to a stop with the needle pointing north.

A DIY SHELTER

Knowing how to build a shelter is an important survival skill. If your tent gets damaged or you are lost in a wilderness environment and can't find the way back to your camp, a DIY shelter will keep you protected from wind, snow, rain, or hot sun. You can keep safe inside your shelter for just a few hours or for a whole night!

If you're in a forest, you can build a **debris** hut in just one or two hours. This type of shelter is made from debris, or materials, such as branches, leaves, tree bark, and **moss**. If you're carrying a jackknife, it will be very useful for cutting branches. It's possible, however, to make this shelter without using any tools at all.

YOU WILL NEED:

- A long, thick, straight branch
- Other assorted branches
- A jackknife (if available)
- Wire, rubber bands, or other binding material from a survival kit
- Debris such as leafy branches, fern leaves, tree bark, and moss

STEP 1: Begin by finding a long, thick, straight branch that will be the hut's ridgepole. When making your hut, try to find material that has fallen onto the forest floor. If you need to cut or break branches off trees, only take what you will use.

STEP 2: To make the hut's frame, create a tripod using the ridgepole and two shorter branches.

You can bind the three branches together using wire or the rubber bands from your survival kit.

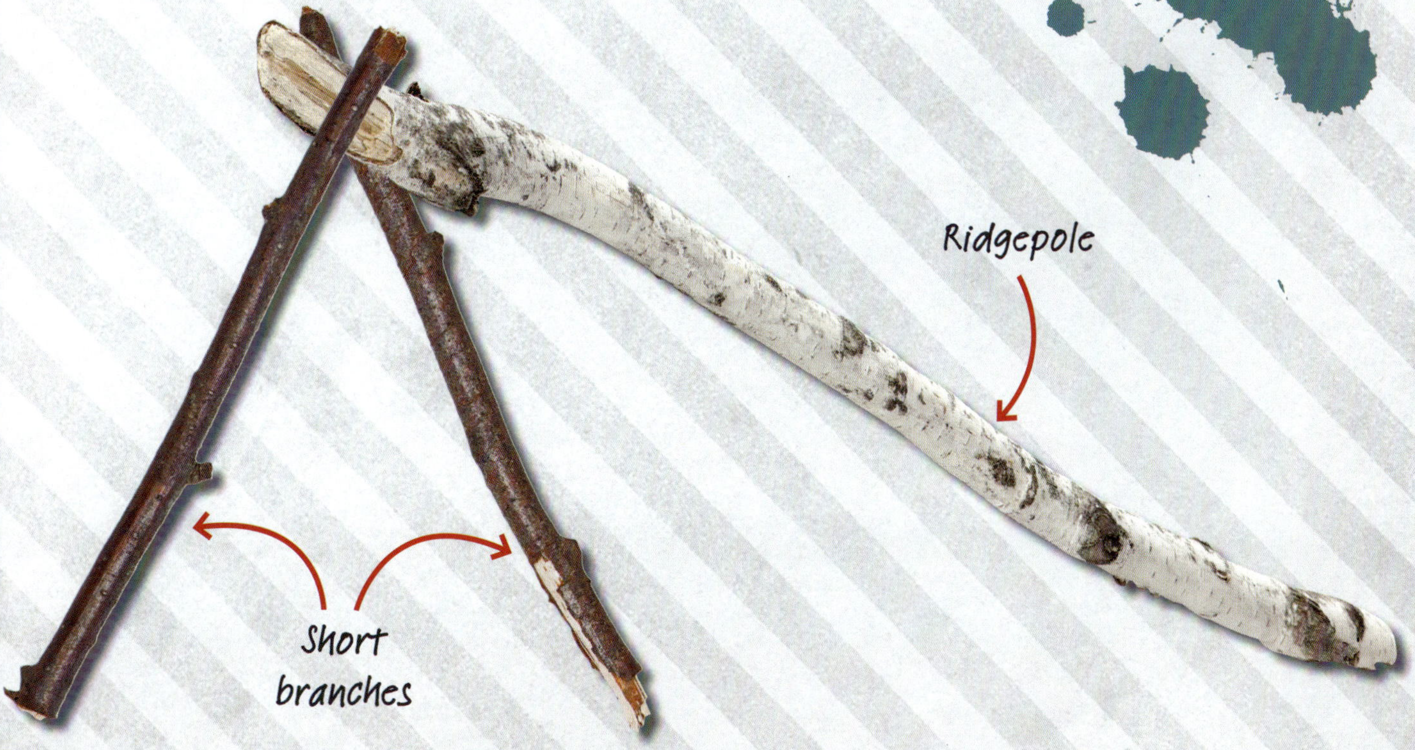

STEP 3: Alternatively, find a tree stump and lean the ridgepole against the stump.

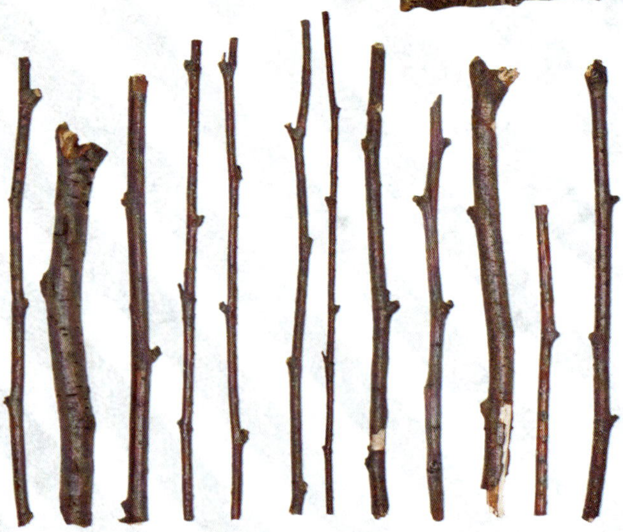

STEP 4: Collect sticks in different lengths.

STEP 5: Prop the sticks along both sides of the ridgepole to create ribbing. The hut's frame is now complete.

STEP 6: Next, gather material, or debris, to cover the frame. Leafy branches, pine tree branches, large fern leaves, bark, and moss all work well.

Bark

Fern leaf

Pine tree branch

Moss

STEP 7: Cover the frame with a thick layer of debris. In a cold weather survival situation, you would need to cover the hut in debris that's about 3 feet (1 m) deep!

STEP 8: Cover the ground inside the hut with leaves and other soft debris.

NO MATCHES CAMPFIRE

A fire can be used for cooking food, boiling water, and keeping warm. You can light a fire with matches, but what can you do if your matches get lost or wet? If this situation crops up in the wilderness, it's possible to start a fire with some paper, a plastic water bottle, and sunlight.

Knowing how to build and start a fire is an important survival skill. You should never try to light a fire without an adult being present, however. Also, did you know that in the United States, nine out of ten **wildfires** are started by people being careless? So if you build a fire outdoors, follow the fire safety rules on these pages. Enjoy using this survival skill, but be responsible, protect the wild places you visit, and stay safe.

YOU WILL NEED:

- A small spade or large flat stone for digging
- Rocks
- Dry grass, leaves, twigs, branches, and logs
- A plastic bottle of water
- A piece of newspaper
- 3 sheets of paper folded in half
- A bucket of water (for putting out the fire)

STEP 1: You will need the sun to be shining in order to light your fire. The sun's light must also be able to easily reach the place where you are working.

STEP 2: Choose a spot to build your fire where there are no trees, plants, or dry grasses within 10 feet (3 m) of the fire.

STEP 3: Clear any debris that might catch fire from a spark, such as dry leaves or twigs, from the 10-foot (3 m) radius of the fire. Save these materials to use as tinder to start the fire.

STEP 4: Dig or scrape a pit in the ground the size you want your fire to be and about 10 inches (25 cm) deep. Surround the edge of the pit with large rocks.

STEP 5: Place the tinder—such as small twigs, dry leaves, grass, and moss—in the bottom of the firepit.

STEP 6: Collect a selection of larger twigs, branches, and logs as fuel for your fire.

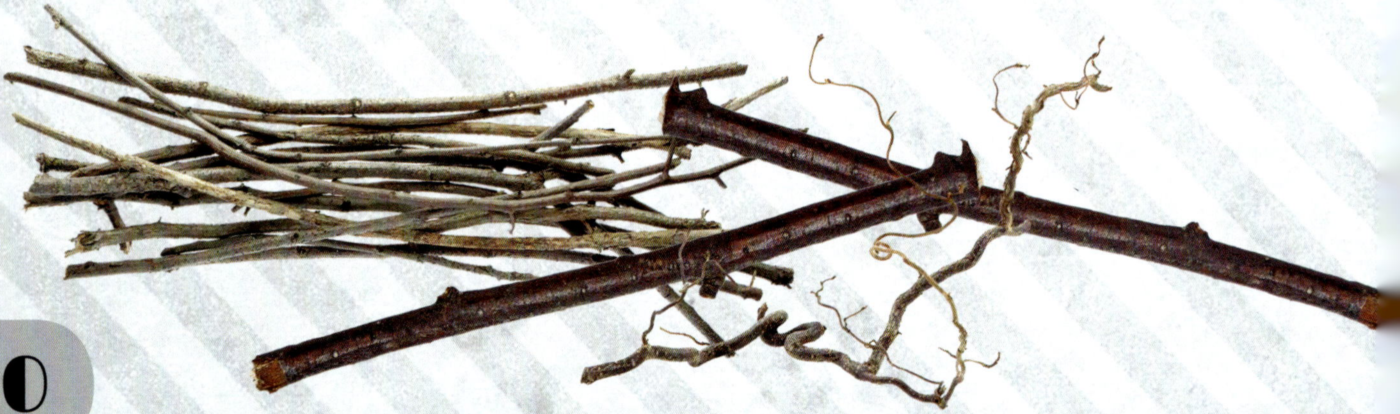

STEP 7: To light the fire, fold a piece of newspaper in half three or four times.

STEP 8: Take the bottle of water and use the rounded end of the bottle to catch the sun's light. Focus it onto the paper, like a magnifying glass. Aim for an area of paper where there is black ink because this will absorb more light.

Within a few seconds, the paper should begin smoldering and a small, smoldering hole will appear.

STEP 9: Once the hole is about the size of a quarter, tuck the newspaper inside one of the folded sheets of paper. When that sheet begins to smolder too, tuck the smoldering papers inside a second and then a third sheet of folded paper.

STEP 10: Finally, gently waft the smoldering bunch of papers from side to side. A flame will appear and as the papers start to burn, carefully drop them into the firepit on top of your dry tinder.

FIRE SAFETY RULES

Always follow these rules when you make a fire.

- Store the wood for your fire upwind and away from the fire, so the wind isn't blowing the smoke toward the wood.
- Never leave a campfire unattended. An adult must stay with the fire at all times.
- Keep a bucket of water near the fire.
- Do not pull sticks or branches out of the fire.
- Always put out a fire by completely soaking it with water. Then stir the remains of the fire and completely soak with water again.
- Make sure the remains of the fire are cold before you leave the fire.

STEP 11: When the small twigs and other dry materials are burning well, add larger twigs and finally branches and logs.

OUTDOOR SOLAR OVEN

Feel like making that all-time camping favorite, s'mores?

You can of course use your survival skills to build a campfire. But you can also try building your own outdoor oven that's powered by the sun.

A **solar-powered** oven can be made from an old file box, aluminum foil, and plastic wrap. The oven can be used to heat soup, beans, or other canned foods—and of course, s'mores!

Let's get building and cooking!

YOU WILL NEED:

- A file box
- A craft knife
- Aluminum foil
- Duct tape
- Sheet of black paper
- Plastic wrap
- A wire coat hanger
- A wire cutter

STEP 1: Ask an adult to help you remove the spring-loaded clip from inside the file box.

STEP 2: Cut a flap in the lid of the box.

STEP 3: Cover the inside of the box with aluminum foil and tape in place.

STEP 4: Place the sheet of black paper inside the box.

STEP 5: Close the lid of the box, leaving the flap outside. Cover the inside of the flap with foil and tape in place.

STEP 6: Stretch plastic wrap over the hole in the box's lid and tape in place.

STEP 7: To cook food in the oven, place the oven in a sunny spot. Open the lid and place the food on the black paper. Then close the lid so the plastic wrap is above the food.

STEP 8: Cut a length of stiff wire from a coat hanger. Tape one end of the wire to the flap. Then position the flap at an angle so that the sun shines onto the foil-covered flap and is reflected into the box. Once the flap is in the best position for capturing sunlight, tape the other end of the wire prop to the box to hold it in place.

STEP 9: Here's how the solar-powered oven works. The sun's light is reflected into the oven, creating heat. Inside the oven, the black paper absorbs the heat. The plastic wrap keeps the heat trapped inside the oven.

Sun reflecting off flap

Food inside box beneath plastic wrap

Wire coat hanger prop

LET'S GET SOLAR COOKING!

HOMEMADE REFRIGERATOR

Would you like to build your own **environmentally friendly** refrigerator for your campsite or backyard? This project shows you how to make a pot-in-a-pot cooler that will keep food and drinks cool. There's no need for electricity. This homemade refrigerator creates its cooling effect using the **evaporation** of water.

STEP 1: Seal up the holes in the bottoms of the flowerpots with duct tape.

STEP 2: Place enough sand in the bottom of the larger pot so that when the small pot is placed inside, the rims of the two pots are level.

STEP 3: Fill the gap between the two pots with sand.

YOU WILL NEED:

- 2 unglazed terra-cotta flowerpots, sized so one fits inside the other leaving a gap
- Duct tape
- Sand
- Water
- A terra-cotta saucer or other shallow dish that covers the top of the smaller pot
- Dish towels

STEP 4: Place your food and drink inside the cooler.

STEP 5: Carefully pour water onto the sand. The sand will soak up the water, so keep pouring until all the sand is soaked, but don't allow it to get sloppy.

STEP 6: Place the saucer on top as a lid, and fill the saucer with water.

STEP 7: Finally, cover the pots with wet dish towels.

STEP 8: Add water to the sand when it dries out. For maximum cooling, keep refilling the saucer and wetting the dish towels too.

The pot-in-a-pot cooler works because the heat outside of the pots will cause the water in the sand to evaporate. As water evaporates, it causes cooling. The temperature inside the pots will be many degrees cooler than outside!

GLOSSARY

anticipate
To think about something in advance and plan for it.

compass
A device that shows you which direction you are traveling in. A compass has a needle that always points north, no matter which direction you are facing.

debris
The remains of something, or broken pieces of something. In a forest, debris might include fallen leaves and broken twigs and branches.

environmentally friendly
Not damaging to the air, land, rivers, lakes, and oceans, or to plants and animals.

evaporation
The process by which liquid water becomes water vapor in the air. Water evaporates when it gets warm.

moss
Low-growing plants that often cover rocks or trees and usually grow in damp places.

solar-powered
Powered by energy from the sun.

survival kit
A collection of items that will be useful in an emergency situation or if a person is camping or living outdoors with few modern comforts. A kit might contain tools, medical equipment, and items used for cooking food.

utilize
To make use of.

wilderness
A wild place where no humans live, such as a desert, forest, or on the slopes of a mountain.

wildfires
Fires in natural habitats such as forests that are sometimes started by lightning, but are often started accidentally by people being careless when building campfires.

READ MORE

Bowman, Chris. *Survive in the Woods*. Minneapolis, MN: Bellwether Media, 2017.

Hewitt, Ben. *The Young Adventurer's Guide to (Almost) Everything*. Boulder, CO: Roost Books, 2019.

Mack, Dave. *Making Shelter in the Wild*. New York: PowerKids Press, 2016.

WEBSITES

www.mosquitomagnet.com/articles/first-time-camping-survival-guide

https://www.wikihow.com/Survive-in-the-Woods

https://smokeybear.com/en/smokey-for-kids

Publisher's note to parents and teachers: Our editors have reviewed the websites listed here to make sure they're suitable for students. However, websites may change frequently. Please note that students should always be supervised when they access the internet.

INDEX